BUFFALO PRAIRIE

based on text by Evelyn Lee
Illustrated by Krista Brauckmann-Towns

Dedicated with love to Bonnie Lee and Emily Lee, two young ladies who are as strong, beautiful, and free-spirited as the flowers of the tallgrass prairie—E.B.L.

My love and thanks to J.T. and Jackie Z. for your ongoing support—K.B.

Book copyright © 2005 Trudy Corporation

Published by Soundprints Division of Trudy Corporation, Norwalk, Connecticut.

Book design: Marcin D. Pilchowski
Book layout: Bettina M. Wilhelm
Editor: Laura Gates Galvin

First Edition 2005
10 9 8 7 6 5 4 3 2 1
Printed in China

Acknowledgements:
    Our very special thanks to Bob Hamilton, Director of Science and Stewardship at the Tallgrass Prairie Preserve, Pawhuska, Oklahoma, for his curatorial review.

Library of Congress Cataloging-in-Publication Data is on file with the publisher and the Library of Congress.

BUFFALO PRAIRIE

based on text by Evelyn Lee

Illustrated by Krista Brauckmann-Towns

Soundprints

Where Children Discover...

One summer day, a young buffalo moves through the prairie with his herd, munching on mouthfuls of grass as he goes.

The sun is hot, and Young Buffalo moves slowly. The grasses barely flutter, but across the sky, clouds begin to gather. A summer storm is on the way!

By late afternoon, clouds fill the sky. Gusts of wind ruffle Young Buffalo's fur and send the grasses into rolling waves. Lightning strikes and thunder rumbles.

Soon, hailstones the size of marbles bounce off the buffaloes' heads and backs. Suddenly, a tornado can be seen on the horizon, swirling toward the herd. It is time to run!

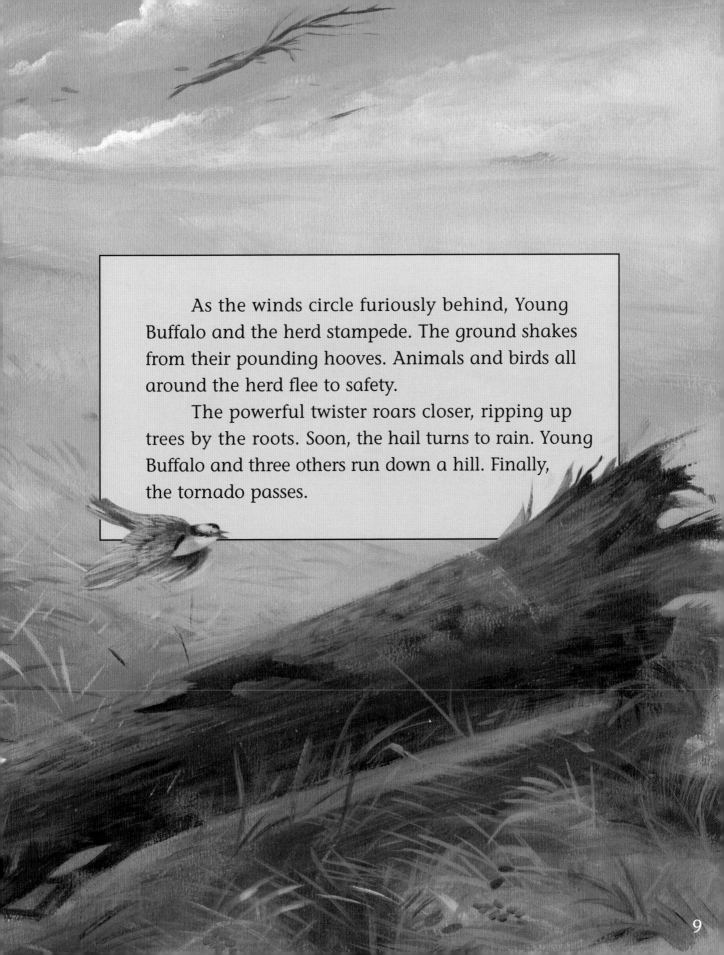

As the winds circle furiously behind, Young Buffalo and the herd stampede. The ground shakes from their pounding hooves. Animals and birds all around the herd flee to safety.

The powerful twister roars closer, ripping up trees by the roots. Soon, the hail turns to rain. Young Buffalo and three others run down a hill. Finally, the tornado passes.

It is calm again. Tree branches and smashed flowers litter the ground.

Young Buffalo and the three others roar, but there is no answer from the rest of the herd. The young ones are alone—for the first time ever.

Young Buffalo and the others search for their herd. They roam for many miles, always grazing on summer grasses.

Several days later, as Young Buffalo and the group walk single file on a dirt trail, Young Buffalo sees a dusty hollow in the ground. He kneels, flops over, and slowly rolls back and forth to cover himself with dust. This rids him of insects. The other buffaloes take turns having a dust bath before they move on.

A whole week passes, and Young Buffalo and his companions are still wandering in search of their herd. All at once, Young Buffalo sees something moving through the prairie grasses!

It is only a coyote, stalking a jackrabbit. The group is safe, but they are still alone. As they patiently plod on, Young Buffalo's keen sense of smell catches a scent from the herd—the other buffaloes cannot be too far!

When Young Buffalo and the others reach the top of a hill, they see black dots scattered in the valley below. They have found the herd!

Young Buffalo trots forward, followed by the other three. Several buffaloes from the herd bellow and plod toward them. They breathe into each other's faces with big snorts of welcome.

Young Buffalo's mother has had a new calf. Young Buffalo now has a new, fuzzy little sister!

By September, Young Buffalo and the herd prepare for the harsh winter ahead. They eat and eat and eat to put on weight, because there will not be much food to find when the snow comes. Young Buffalo's fur begins to grow long and sleek to help keep him warm in the coming months.

In autumn, the days grow cooler and shorter. Young Buffalo and the herd walk through drying grasses, eating wild rye and sedges that grow green in the cooler season.

There are short afternoon storms, but the rainwater dries quickly and the tall grasses become drier than ever.

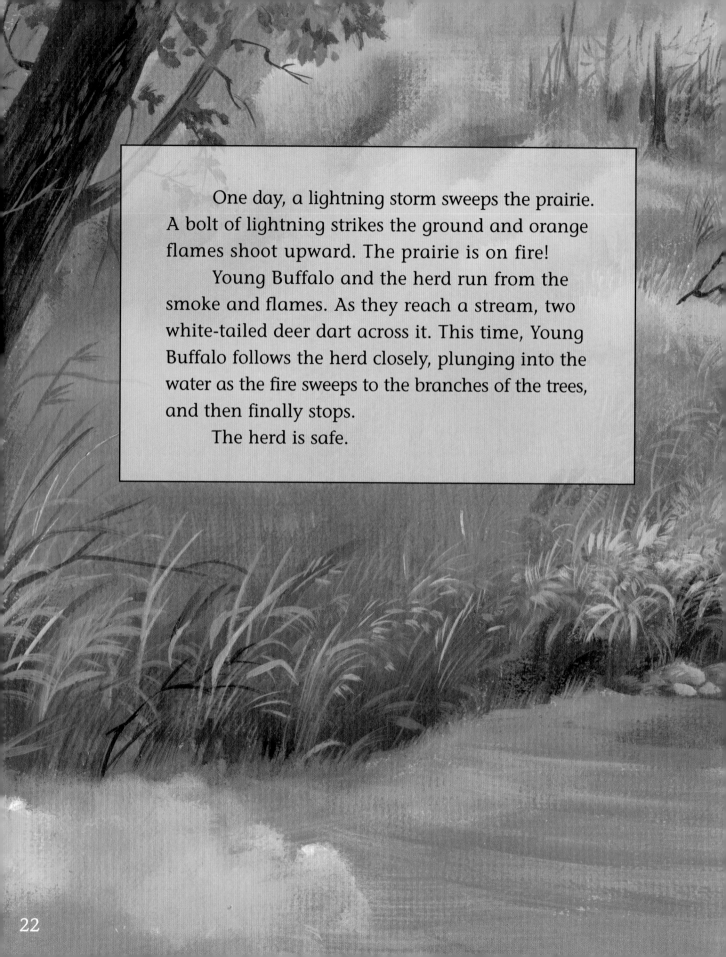

One day, a lightning storm sweeps the prairie. A bolt of lightning strikes the ground and orange flames shoot upward. The prairie is on fire!

Young Buffalo and the herd run from the smoke and flames. As they reach a stream, two white-tailed deer dart across it. This time, Young Buffalo follows the herd closely, plunging into the water as the fire sweeps to the branches of the trees, and then finally stops.

The herd is safe.

As the days grow even chillier and shorter, the large herd splits up. Young bulls form bachelor groups. Big, older bulls go off by themselves. Young Buffalo and his three companions stay in a small herd. His mother and his baby sister are in another herd with his older sister.

One morning, Buffalo awakens to cold air and a gray sky. The world feels still. Snow is coming!

Flakes of snow begin to gather on Young Buffalo's thick, dark coat. Puffs of steam billow from his nostrils in the frosty air. Together with his new herd, Young Buffalo is ready to face the harsh winter. And together they will wait for spring when the first green shoots of grass will poke out of the thawing earth.

THE BUFFALO LIVES IN NORTH AMERICA

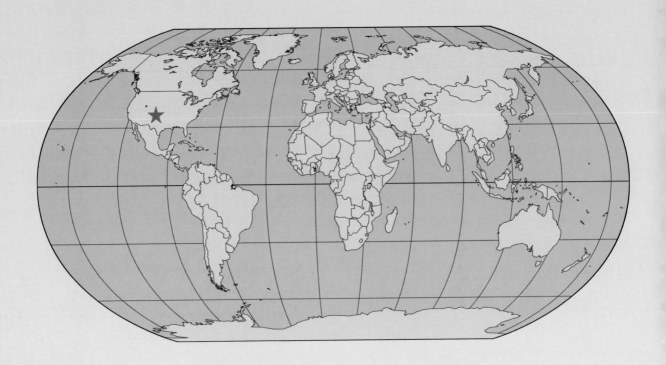

ABOUT THE BUFFALO

The buffalo depicted in this story is called the American Buffalo. The American Buffalo is actually a bison.

American Buffaloes are the heaviest land animals in North America. Buffaloes are up to 6 feet tall and can weigh up to a ton—that's 2,000 pounds! For such large animals buffaloes can run surprisingly fast—up to 30 miles an hour.

Buffaloes are plant eaters and their diet consists mainly of grass, twigs and shrubs. They swallow their food without chewing it.

▲ Dragonfly

▲ Bur Oak

▲ Black-eyed Susan

▲ Jackrabbit

▲ Pale Purple Coneflower

▲ Fox Squirrel

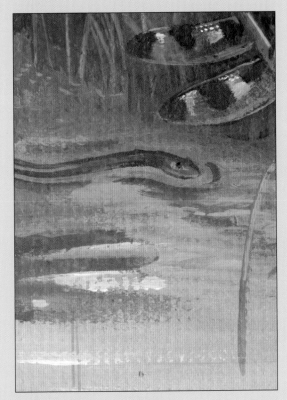

▲ Rough Green Snake

▲ White-tailed Deer

▲ Wild Turkey

▲ Eastern Collared Lizard

▲ Eastern Meadowlark

▲ Red-tailed Hawk

PICTORIAL GLOSSARY

▲ Buffalo

▲ Coyote

▲ Raccoon

▲ Greater Prairie Chicken